# The Crushing Organ

# The Crushing Organ

*poems by*

## Dan Rosenberg

Dream Horse Press
California

**Dream Horse Press**
www.dreamhorsepress.com
Editor: J.P. Dancing Bear

Dream Horse Press
Post Office Box 2080
Aptos, California 95001-2080
U.S.A.

Rosenberg, Dan
          the crushing organ
                    p.80


                    ISBN 978-1-935716-19-8
                    1. Poetry

10 9 8 7 6 5 4 3 2 1

First Edition

Cover: "As my soul fades away" by Shahram Alizadeh
http://soulcollector13.deviantart.com/

# Table of Contents

# III.

*the body preserves*
*its world*

Inger Christensen

I.

# MY FIELD

Seeing my field sometimes makes me cry.
I cry when bits of my field get blown
into my eyeball. They scrape me up.
I want the roots to hold it all down.
I want the sun to be potent and kind.
I wear just enough plaid. One stalk is not
a harvest here, where the perfect field
is so thick with life it forms a higher field,
a vibrant plateau—a wall? No, it is too deep
to be a wall. I press against the thresher
with my hip. Hello little squirrel, have you
seen such density before, you'll never
go hungry again, new seeds grow legs
they choose to use for standing still.
This is the end to all worry and purpose.
It could have been otherwise but isn't.
Wet mouth hanging, one drunken farmer
in a thick field can't do much damage.
This corn is over my head and sharp;
running through the field I'm whipped
all over by a cat-o-countless-tails.
I would have been a terrible sailor.
I would have followed the boat in my own
dinghy, collecting the planks as they fell
to the wake. Rebuild, rebuild, the problem
of identity: a minefield all rusted shut.
Tiny plants are growing from the mines.
Everywhere is the same when I'm speaking.

It doesn't matter what you say to plants,
just breathe on them. They are symbiotes.
They thrive when you thrive. Rabbits,
spiders, prairie dogs all make my field
shiver; I'd press them to my mouth
if I could. I'd bring them inside.

## I'M WITH YOU

My lip was overflowing. Faster than the sea
could keep up: Three jackals conversed
under trees with their backs turned.
Some kind of bird fell dead at their paws.
Then the fragile table setting came to me
in a whole picture, as necessary. Curtains
flanked the radiant windows for a day's fraction.
Wire mesh formed a ginger cup which too
had its uses. I understood the discarded casings,
dropped husks curled, beckoning
over their empty centers. If only to rub my hands
over the earth. My inside-out hands.
Two people on a raft in the lumbering river
came to me as lovers but they were only friends.
Of course, I could have smelled their picnic
from anywhere. I felt suddenly great,
then more than a thousand soldiers fell apart
through my fingers. Emptied themselves.
Not even what I sat on was preserved.
Slowly pulling me toward one more center.
I started humming two songs at once:
one of first roots and one of second rings.

# HAIR

*"Sins in a nett I seke to hold the wynde"*
　　　　　-Sir Thomas Wyatt

I came to, feeling broke

about the head,

a crown of spoons in my hair.

Funny, I hadn't thought myself

thick enough still for all this

eating and being eaten.

At the party of miraculous drugs

I'd been teetotaling my way along:

Repeatedly sniffed past,

I knew everyone

was behind me with fogged spoons

hanging from their noses.

The rest of the night was a blurry string

of stop signs worn

like a choker around

the neck of an Italian girl.

She posted herself at every corner:

*Noli me tangere.*

Spooning the hostess I told her

the party of miraculous drugs

was behind me, with a nose

hanging from its disgusting face.

She started feeding spoonfuls of drugs

into my hair. She fed

the Italian girl into my hair.

The stop signs curled

like burnt paper, red,

they split my ends.

14

I had to lie down
under the miraculous bed,
my head pressed flat to the floor.
I felt her shift above my temples,
surreptitiously tickling
her own nose. I couldn't even
roll on my side,
so heavy was my hair. I thought,
I'll always have her up there,
sated and tender in a tangle.

# RECOVERING

My brief foray into silence
left me chapped to my ends
and alone with the carrion birds.
One turned to me
with a face half missing.
One turned to me
from the third chamber run dry.
I felt as if my mouth had turned
against me, uneasy
sloughing off its skin.
Feathers were all
I could see of the sky, folded,
slowly making room for sunrise.

\*

From the east a bird turned
to me with my bright hand
in its mouth. The bird had
no tongue. The light of my hand spoke
in tiny wattages.
The bird suffered two small holes
in its beak. With my mouth
to them, I tasted the tension
of my hand clenched
down on light. A white stream
of breath broke out.

# MICROBURST

I.

This is the end result
of someone else's party.
The socks can't tell
which side is outside
and my shirt is a hole
in light. Some things are known
only by their limits,
some can't be stared into
or out of. The slick heart
of the sun. The sun's
turbulent heart.
In the party of our system
I'm eccentric on the outskirts
and declassified, a limit
repeatedly breached.
I swing close to what
I want to see, say *hey*,
I touch an arm and the arm
doesn't jiggle. It's
a banister. My voice
fits into the dance beat
like a name
on a grain of rice.
Fits so well not even I
can hear it, or taste.

II.

I name every lobster
I see. I've eaten
a crab from its own skull.
I've nursed a bunny
into a slower death,
drowned a spider
too thick to catch
or crush. Some things
are just too messy
to end in the usual ways.
I hold a snow globe
of New York to a toddler:
She strikes like a snake.
She strikes like a match.
The snake's head is a flame.
If I don't name you
you don't survive.

III.

The heavens are bleached out
with streetlights and we all feel
larger. I step up
to a blasted tree still
circulating its sap in open air.
The ants have begun
their reclamation work.
The trunk extends
its innards like a fan.
The tree's slices of heart
reflect my hand's heat;
what I'm feeling out
is my own pulse, translated.
I don't speak this capillary
language, like guts wanting
to wrap themselves in skin.
I'm just here to note.
I note the microburst
stepped down from above
our false upper limit
and swiped my street in lashes.
I note myself crawling
into and under the opened pines.
These pits once held roots.

# BLASON

Midnight never ended with the sun
still unlit above her narrow cheek.
She was floating when decay began
to spread her piece by piece.
Her hair in thirsty nets caught up
the teeth of sound and squeezed
water from them, dropped them
to her hands. She threw her hands
into a growing weave, her ears
against the matted empty, her eyes
to the distance from herself.
She threw her blood and bones
to the closeness; unhooked, her skin
fell and spread like a reprimand.
Everywhere there was a mess of life.
Her hands gave birth to trees,
snaking into each other, starving
as a gross possessive lover. Her ears fell
to the green hunger, to the sound
of thrashing, bodies mashed against
each other, chewing her dust to new
black earth, while her two eyes paced
back and forth above it all. The churning,
the spray of her like dandruff,
then what were her many parts
fell into life, began their slow settling.

# YOU CAN'T STAY ALONE

*after Amichai*

You can't stay alone
and the lights are all on timers.
But sometimes I'm reading
and a shadow passes by the window
looking sidelong like a person.

You can't stay alone
and you have to bend the wire hanger
into the shape of a human heart,
and you have to replace your heart.

Every night I have this dream:
My teeth fall out, exposing metal roots
which start to burn, and if I stop talking
they will set this planet on fire.
There will be no whimper even.

When I wake up I walk the beach, trace
a sand crab's path into the shoreline,
feed and hide in the intertidal.
But you must not stay alone.

Though sometimes my mouth goes dry
and my tongue is an ambulance
rushing to someone who's already dead,
my hand still closes around yours:
a grasp, a greeting, a letting go.

# I AM

I am the final tissue, the one
most steeped in divinity.

Sometimes I am one of those cups,
the only ones allowed in the heart.

I am painted brightly to catch the eye
in a mist of my own breath.

I am the accordion note.
I have a mane and ribbons
roaming inside me. I know
how to use, how to be

used in a crowd.
I am that part of the rug.
The empty center of the apple.

With the rabbis closing in, riding my wake
over the United—over the Earth—and
my hips, door, my islands

and fog press the air.
My sloth, my tree,
my tree sloth
filled with voice.

# NEW IDIOMS

When the night is fully formed
but your pulse has the cadence of anticipation.
Loving and hating something simultaneously.
Cracking a pomegranate open
to find nothing but mist and hunger.
The pleasure of never having enough.
Homecoming to a place you've never been,
then remembering your daughter,
always afraid of new illnesses.
When you catch a spider in your fist,
take it out of your house and release it,
knowing your hand will feel dirty forever.
When you catch a spider in your fist
and hear the sound of laughter down the hall.
Your brain's sadness trumped by some
strange bird calling for his lover.
When your family surrounds you,
how grateful to be embarrassed by them.
The way Matryoshka dolls replace
psychology when the lights go out,
and how you can never find the smallest doll.
Sleeping behind a wall with no ears.
The secret lust for rainfall.
When you're left without a seam,
tiny, with no more empty spaces.
Your heavy club foot scatters your tracks.
The varied populations of the cusps.

Being born a dry orphan but finding
a tongue to call your own.
Speaking as if poorly of the dead.

# DEAR BODY

Though I don't think of you as separate
you thread your screws into me anyway.
Tender body, what basic state are you in?
Where should you be watered? Body,
the ache of your proscenium pulls tight
against your softness and your hardness.
Gods have no words for body, and thus
when bodies come they never know.
Ghost of a body, your body will not end.
Before plants were first crushed to paper
a man gave body to fear and was killed.
When the area code sleeps our bodies
get up to touch each other. My body
fingers letters on the body of my neighbor:
Me, over and over. Me, Me, Me.

# PURPOSE

Giving up on the day, I climb to the roof
and spread-eagle. Birds choose
a representative to peck out my liver,
but I'm not interested in the role.
Go away. The gold capitol dome
feeds the clouds like a giant nipple.
The clouds are no single thing.
I'm worried that my blood will go
where it must, completely unaddressed.
How can I be heard inside myself?
The shingles flap like mouths,
pathetic toothless mouths. I want
to cover them all. If I spread myself
thin enough, I can go totally limp
and their charades of speech will move me.
From high above, I might be said to ripple.

# AT THE CATHOUSE

Seven kinds of leopard splayed,
and within each leopard a smaller,
more subtle ear pressed my pulse.
Every *you're the one* rebounded

its course around my vascular shame.
I stayed wholly present, my shame
left crying off a clothes-line.
The leopards set me awry,

toothy guideposts with new gravity.
Undulation, I passed over you again,
and again your sensual maw became
a paradigm of weaving with the right

and unraveling with the left. Then
your lame prey conjured herself
in a shroud of mist, and I choked
as if I was fully constituted. The image

of *what you want* appeared with fingers
slender as a wave of knives. From some
inner darkroom I turned my eyes to them
as the leopards breathed out black light.

# BLOOD DIAMONDS

Never trust your first birth.
The green-tinted window renders
all things both sickly and alive.
How straight is a natural spine?
What colors do your eyes impose?
You couldn't bruise an onion
with a pickaxe, but your wit
broke us through to wetter skins.
We pulled the leaves from pinecones
to rediscover who we loved.
Food arrived and we ate it.
Drinks arrived and we splashed
as if for victory. Understand,
we were very young. Our palms
were stripped of lines. Clean now,
I've lost my will for self-defense,
so I crack my teeth open for you.
Inside is nothing but blood
and nerves. To offer up yourself
is a form of pain. My teeth crumble
like starving buds. Not even chalk
can be more white. Full of whole
colors, my picture of you cannot
be folded in a stone. So I squeeze
tight, squeeze until you drip away.

# INTERVIEW

Have you eaten?
Yes, of the roots.

But is the body not now dying?
Inasmuch as it was a fire.

Beforehand?
The beginning is bitten.

And what is an apple, then?
Outside the lines, uncooperative child.

Who holds the pencil?
God holds the pencil.

What do you hold to be true?
Not every creature yawns when I yawn.

Are you tired?
The volcano nods before it rises.

Have you seen a crater lake?
Carbonation belches unholy in a field of dead cattle.
It casts a withering net.

And who is there with you?
I can't turn my head. I have
no concept of restraint.

Then what's straight ahead?
An ember breathed into, the flicker
immaterial, it could be a fruit
or fist, the boiling crawl of veins.

Are you a child? A hungry child?
My mouth is a nest
you fail to thicken.

To a state of belief?
Not even when I've laid my hands
to rest on your throat.

You seem unsettled.
But every brain's in chambers.
Even the brain of disaster.

You seem very unsettled.
In my brain a black-eyed deer
gnaws at the staples in a telephone pole.

Do you dream of blue light?
Do you carry my voice in your hair?

# HERE

Here's the word for an ant's single leg.

I plucked it and breathed it.

I caught it beneath my gum line.

Here are some plants I grew by speaking to them.

Here are the aphids that happened when my mind wandered.

I was babbling; I'm sorry.

I said the sap would be as blood, as coveted.

The sap was as blood, the wet of it.

I set a few rules and broke them.

Some spiders can resurrect themselves.

Call it a miracle when I do that.

Call it a mitochondrion, I said.

Call it symbiosis.

Here's how you're my children.

Here's how I made your lungs insufficient.

Here's how I filled your lungs with bacteria.

I needed a place to put them.

I wanted you to have them.

I am in complete control of my dreams.

I let them be this way.

My dreams fall on cracks and grow.

There is excess to my mind and I throw it down the cracks.

Here's a brown spot on an ovary.

Here's the brown globe stumbling through autumn.

II.

# BROTHER

Brother you saw the pine tree depress itself
against the window. It collected our leanings.
Listing in the house of crooked corners,
we were just children carving our claims
into the earth we never questioned.
And when I crawled in your shadow
you dimmed the sky, stayed up
close to the sun, spread your silhouette
on the landscape. When I could run
there was nothing before me but a sloped oval
of track to tread. The bleachers bore
your name. I was stupid with pride. I was
always the ant infected by a lancet fluke,
compelled up a blade of grass, my mandible
my only grounding. I clamped my body's
white flag to your field, brother. What else
presented itself so fully to the visible world?

# DIVINITY IS POWER AND LOVE, MARTY

Under the stoplight the desperate lady glows green.
The vole by the road squeaks for a baseboard,
a container, afraid. Distended and trembling,

her body, an old boot fattened full of rain.
And God pulls on her hair to make it grow

a little. I step to the sidewalk and age
terribly in the long gasp before she breaks
and bleeds on a jagged fender. A dandelion

spreads its seeds to the asphalt
like hairy fallen stars. The slowly dying
have awful names: Elizabeth, Marty.

Elizabeth—I touch her hand, I am
marked. I bear a black dot. And God pulls
his own hair. Only the black dot breathes.

It is almost singing from my palm. The dot
drags threads through my hand like it knows my

future. I'm on the rim of endless witnessing,
charting its limits. At times I tilt my head
over the edge, feel my brain's watchful quadrant

pulling away like a slow boat. God is
my mooring line; he starts crumpled but flattens.

# ORIGINS

The stop sign
makes stops, starts.

Wire becomes
serpent when

it sparks. To speak,
exhale. It exits.

To exist,
be a serpent

coiled, not curled.
To strike,

bite the outlet
with a bright

face of teeth.
To talk. A tree.

All hanging
is wall hanging.

The wall drops
the roof.

# SCRIPT

Today I woke up in a storm
reflected in my sheets as if
I'd dreamt it. The pillows I'd bought
for support now have me surrounded.
The heater casts its red eye
about the room. I'm always afraid
of what's behind me: The truck
bearing down, this violent bed.
The refrigerator is plotting
under cover of thunder.
At least the ceilings are high.
Some water damage up there looks
like a city reflecting itself in a lake.
I'm always wanting what's not
in front of me. To be a squirrel
is to be so light the trees you leap on
can't feel you. There are no whites
to their eyes. I'm never one of them.
I'm too heavy. My back sinks
into the mattress, my limbs askew.
Some storms have eyes, can take
your roof away. It's happened
here before, left my apartment
stained and populated. Now
I'm only afraid of the sky,
the way I can feel it reading me.
But I don't really mind. I'm
an ideogram. Just by moving my arms
I tell some kind of story.

# COMMUNION

The sun daggers at our legs
but can't get to our eyes.
Our nerves cut on each drifting plate.
A bud abandons its colors,
snaps in sneaker treads,
while three clouds lick each other
like sappers digging
into the same ground—
how all things meet is warfare
when beautiful. So far from here.
Wicker the parent's wrinkling face.
If you throw away your lust
for eternal life, you forgotten landmine,
you evergreen constantly dropping
into pots of glue, you will begin
a transformation. Try to remember
being chased. Then an apple rotting.
Then one towel thread crying—
flat on the field of dead towels—
hackling up its dusty wisps.
Dark room, empty, with spotlight.
Purple your fingertip
with a thready noose. Frayed
speaker wire with its mouth
taped shut, caught up
in its own spindle, what's left
of all the vertical cities?
The sun as a salty eraser

wiped the cities down to glass.
Some ashes bury trees,
some cup their roots. Hard water
bursts fountain-high, from your spigot
to from my mouth.
From my mouth a wet strand
traces a brittle hook.
Then the hook is a snake,
methodically stabbing its own heel.

# EAT THE BONES OF THE WORLD

Eat the bones of the world
like an unnatural mouth
in the tricky posture of opening.

The air stains your breathing
with cow manure smells
on a western wind. So stop.

Be no cattle nor cattle hand.
So eat the radiant bones,
the girding of the world.

In the growth of tailored pines.
In the corner cemetery. The road
cut into the bones of the world

so low you drive level
with the dead. You live
downhill from the dead

but they don't sing to you.
You live downhill from someone
else's dead and you must

eat the bones of the world
with your last tooth some day.
Some day with both fists

in a pantomime of giddy fire.
Some day you'll wake up
in the revenant springtime

and eat the unforgiving bones,
morning to marrow, a dog
who licks the whipping hand.

# BECK AGAIN
*after Šalamun*

The largest spinning jenny still couldn't
stop me. The chair is designed for subservience.
My shoulders are too broad for a box, even

a refrigerator box. My fingertips are peach pits.
Their ridges were intended. They were crafted.
One such artist refused the sun, and his face

left its mark on the future. His pants
were all over each other. Then the burning stopped.
Then the burning was childless. England

will be the first to go, then the shedding will quench
the homeless. The tortoise is immoral. Airplane
droppings can be transparent. Shells are

for people too, and after my pets are sullied
I unzip my interlocking verbs. Give me
your highbeams. Open to air. Lost pestle,

which desert insect can redeem you? And break
your taste for prognosis, while below the temple rivers
split their mouths. Incans saw the Spanish plague.

Abandoned gods become mosquitoes. At last
your factory has come, at last the lancet
is a world. Sympathy cards muffle themselves

in the garden. Come closer, dry stamp. I
haven't seen your homeland. We'll ask
the president for one more revolution.

# CONTRA

The filament in the light bulb is my brother.
I have tall aspirations; their buildings
have hallways that extend to points of light.
A drop of blood becomes a person,
according to certain government agencies,
and you are no mother to only children.
You've mirrored the inside of my head:
Stand in my center and I am surrounded,
beneficent circle of you. I want to break
a record or a frequency, inputting our generational
code for extra lives in Contra: a series
of oppositions: up and down, left and right,
B and A; twice I have fallen from a tree as if
it birthed me, spotting a face passing by in the bark;
twice I have climbed up missing her footholds.
This is America and I am pixilated with love.
My thumbs are bulbous, like smaller versions
of what I imagine a rutabaga looks like. At times
I don't fit this body, and at times the doors
slamming down the hall require my attention.
I'm back. I know a rutabaga is a Swedish turnip.
Sometimes I'm shocked by the simplest things:
They grow something in Europe named summer rape,
use it for bird feed, and rapeseed oil is used
often as a lubricant. Compatible partners
need similar sensibilities. You need help.
You precede the dark glass. Unsure

of his home, a spider starts to build
a new one in the corner. Now he's dead
and I'm twitchy with guilt, darling, are you
sure? It's two in the morning and I'm distant,
killing spiders. Shake me and you'll hear
a rattle. Run a current through me;
I won't light up enough for you to read by.

# FRACTURING AS A KINDNESS TO BE MINED

Couple blunting the edge of *I love you*,
you hammer each other home

against the full range of color:
the doorframe, the domestic honeycomb

opening itself, unfurling to the flat
pastels of couple. You burnish each other

nightly as abutting doorknobs.
To resurrect: to shake the ant farm,

the reproductive will. Couple, unclench
your nudity; stand no longer naked

at the microwave reheating. Offer
more silence, less backwash masquerading

as communion. Not forbidden,
not whetted inside a moonstone.

# HOW DO WE AVOID LIVING IN JERSEY?

I meant to say
something else entirely to you

listen, I have no gauges, what is Jersey
but an island of holes filling

sometimes I forget to breathe then lightheaded
there you are

in the Hudson river
fishermen drop sparkling threads

you slip in your earrings
& my mouth opens to your throat

to get not around but through Jersey
bite down on a pomegranate seed

# WHAT'S THERE

There's seeing the girl and there's seeing her
switch to a seat farther from you.
There's a red bird and there's a cardinal
freaking from the shrub
to the power lines so quickly
he's a bright stitch tying the sky
down. Your one vest has just
two buttons strung up with lots
and lots of brittle threads. When
your oven timer fails you yet again
and the firemen put out your supper
just like they did almost every Sunday
for your grandmother who fed you
the thin strip of roast that was neither raw
nor charred, you feel ready
for the public. You watch yourself
in shop windows and there's a walk
and apparently there's a strut
you've never seen. Your father
is a caretaker and your mother
is a caretaker. It takes you forever
to sign off when chatting with your
neighbor. Your acronyms fail you
as they refuse to be quicker
than the full-fleshed sentiment.
There's a field you can mark up
with your footprints and there's nothing

at all. Your ghost is a battery and some kind
of GPS for your body; it drives you
and you welcome the mechanical
voice. It needs a key to get it going.
There it is, going. Everyone takes care.

# MOTHER TONGUE

Her voice strikes the sky's white comfort.
Mice burrow through her bones.
The flag of our country trips an alarm.
Threads in the dirty laundry separate.
My father leans against his horse,
the flank, closes his eyes, breathes
through his teeth. And the water rises,
approaching his eyebrows,
it wants something, maybe to see.
It is getting too bright outside.
She is surrounded by candles with black wicks.
The roaches are afraid; their legs flutter
in the air, slowly, slowly.
The boats are on fire.
She says my balloons are full of poison.
Where is my blue towel?
She says the telephone lines are noosing.
Where is my collection of blue threads?
Her fingers, thinning their way toward me.
The curtains are bursting.
My throat empties. She steps past me,
I see her toes, I see her tail. My ears
are pierced, my blood is silver, reaching out.
The grass sharpens against itself.

# AT FLOWER, GRIPPING

Epistle, a yellow footprint on the hardwood. Open the fist, a palm. A shake. Nine walnuts in a Ziploc baggie chatter. I'm holding. I'm shaking. My photograph slinks down. Its frame. Frayed like shoelace. Her lips purse. Every edge threatens a fall. Even hems, even lips, even beauty's tight edge. I'm pressing against. The factory atop my neck. The spill. One flash surprises, the next captures. I freeze wide open. It's a countdown. If thunder comes. Chewing comes easily. Yellow my finger in the lily. It doesn't keep to itself. As well it should. Woman in bra between dogwoods. Red spills on her head. Just a magazine ad. A dangle. A docile puppy in a nook. A shoulder. I've fallen. Not my nook. Limpid with springtime my angles. Shake, a greater tremble. Tremble my ginger veins. A color wheel of fingers. Pointing, a basement before dawn. The chimney a finger. What she wants. My eyes, then the frame. Then my chest. A descent. A cracked cocoon. No moth. Bulbs in the basement open. It takes forever. Petals fall, her feet. Recover the ants all together. Light, then hand, then wall. Thumb become. Touch. A mandible. My crushing organ. My outreach. A small apple falls. The worm inside. What eats. What's eaten. Two flowers kiss, wilt. The cyclist falls. The garbage is a nest.

# REASON FOR SURRENDER

Long Island again, in the yellow-light time of year:
Your family home juts up like a silty arm.

The dead have no reason to eat,
but they eat. The horizon crumples like fire.

Long Island smelling of your grandmother
in the last hospital days. The drip won't stop

until it stops. You want to say, "The cathedral is a dildo."
You can't trace the reason of your own mouth,

the wet path around home. And you swing
the front door shut like a hammer. Their faces.

"Our past is bracing for some blow,"
you want to say, your feet scraped clean

on the family carpeting. You pile too much
on the edge of the fall. Red-veined maple leaves

leave. They sway into the pool and curl. The grown woman
is a shopper, not a sister. Long Island air

pollinates your head. You remember a sparrow's nest.
It crumples and turns. Familiar faces. The cankerworms

silk down from the canopy like psychoactive pills
slugging down your throat.

# IF IT'S NOT COMING IT MUST BE GOING AWAY

Drop the slow winter jacket
to the floor. I pray for the cold
to stay in it forever. In six months
I will still be young and forgetting
winter. New trees will slice
my fingers open. Trees will spill out.
But for now I have somehow
placed my insides on the surface.
A train whistles and my redbreast
collapses. Nobody can see her,
but we all hear the whistle. Ice thickens
the pond each night. Each day I find
a fat rhombus of sun and stay
on its edge. The sidewalk seems
unreasonably happy, and I've lived here
longer than I've been alive,
so slowly does time leak
into this town. In winter
I conceive of the trees and am
surprised to be a supporter
of snow, a center, a core of value.
We come so close to absolute
zero we nearly stop our atoms
in their shivering. Or the reverse:
one foggy bowl of soup
heating my motion all night
on the porch with visible breath.

Everything exposed
becomes a border full of open doors.
Impure. When I leap
off the edge of my porch I believe
in the ground below to fall to.
I believe in the ground
below that as well.

# WHAT HOME

The ship is a growing ash.
It slides into the dock's artery.

Dragging a blanket of light,
the sun leans into water.

Your mitten empties
from my hand. Under a lattice

of wind, my hair lashes out.
Your silhouette

scrapes the bumps from my skin.
I breathe in what you've left

behind. My own exhale
spills to my chin and into

the visible cold.
Your footsteps hammer out

some pulse. The ship is no longer
on fire. The ship is home.

Strips of black tire
push it back at the sea.

# III.

# RECAPITULATE

This time I'll stay in the womb.
Won't slip onto solid ground,
umbilical cord trailing like the whip
between a man and his last horse.

This time I won't be blue and near-blind
in the unbelievable slop and drain
and scream of becoming one more
breather with a mouth more of teeth

than tongue. No longer a nub splitting
into myself, clinging to her, an inner
lump, leeching. I'm no creature
anymore, see me breathe, filling in

my form, my teeth like tiny flairs.
Mother, forgive me these strokes,
this growth I've teethed, this drove
against my own mount, unwarranted,

but the hand that feeds *de facto* smells
of meat. The natal dam demands
an eventual breach: See my fingers, see me
frame a cage; against my mother's ribs

my fingers frame a cage of shadows.
Then a rabbit with uneven ears, liberated,

then dissolving. In the twists of my hands
I see at last a person is no state of being

but a force, pushing. My mother fed me
and I grew. I grow. My life stripped
from her inner movements, all her pills
sped up into confetti, sustaining her,

some replacement, and I am grateful
for this macular site, for my emergence,
for this dark space in my mother's eye
where I am never born.

# SUGAR GLIDER

I'm no swimmer but I can skim. A fat mile
of water flaps between us like a beggar's

self-directed maledictions. It beats
the ground under a frayed curtain of clouds

hanging up to dry around the sun. These days
taste endless on my tongue. I come down

hard on the rhododendrons, feet pacing
my property in the mitigated light until the horizon

clamps its lonely fever down on me. I'm not
healthy all night, curled on one side and shivering.

Come here, where light drools on my face
while I make excuses for myself, for how hurried

the sun was to get here, for how the world is
a set of damp and mismatched jaws.

I think we fit in the cracks between the teeth.
Together, a sour residue, the slow corroding,

the irreparable spill. I toe gingerly into the water,
you turn away, my little blood pump jumps.

# EXEUNT OMNES

When only two ways to go.
The law of excluded middle:
x is or is not the case. As in,
Lover descended the sun
or Lover thrown open
the trap like a minaret.
Two mice in constant panic,
the same as two mice. Being
unforgivable Lover removes
her dark glasses, dark in here,
sunless, night. Post-op mice
spinning wheels like thinking,
how many rotations per light bulb?
Energy from spinning, energy
from splitting or sticking together—
to cleave—Lover bent
like a backdrop. One mouse
per fist a live performance:
stage right, stage left, two
curtains closing. Lover
squeaks cagey, licks a wet
metal ball. Or Lover gloved,
needles and drugs. Smiling
teeth bright under red lights,
Lover decapitated by curtain,
head rolling her left or mine.

# RESUSCI ANNIE

Resusci Annie


Caroling in your fiberglass my mouth
fails, another abortive slit for me to save.
I have imbued your body with life and you
have no legs, Annie, what's happened
to our capacity for love? It ripples slack
against your torso, a t-shirt dreamed up
for someone more complete.

Don't unseal my little humiliations;
bleach left in water reduces to rotten
water in time. Clean one, why can't I
retain your eyes? Like night terrors
some things refuse us, the sturdy ones.

Annie I put the mask on you. Annie
the hot and wet of me could sheen along
your face until the lightning bugs return;
tilt back your plastic chin and breathe.

## Test Dive

Slumped as if cut-stringed in the bar booth,
Annie, why'd I bring you here? Smoke leaks
through your jaw like a horrible lust unhinged

but I can't stop looking, Annie, we've come
to be filled or aired out I know but you seem
more complete than hollow now. One waitress

wonders at your empty sleeves; I reach over,
avert your eyes. Annie how am I supposed
to let you be? Fill yourself with life,

Annie, she's coming back with beers.
I reach down, check: My legs are still there.
You nest yourself in a smoky abdomen, flat

snap of metal where your heart should be.
A poster on the wall wants us to expose
ourselves, Annie why not this once?

I press against your chest to hear it pop.
In my several days' stubble I find one
of your hairs, Annie, is this a gift or evidence?

## Test Ride

We've put the hazards on but they're
not coming, Annie, what white damage
have you done? No passersby, nobody

but me saying your name like peeling
an orange, the sweet and sticky breeze.
It leaves my laundry wet for days.

Here a slow strobe fills your jaw
with yellow light, an even glow.
We are so much open space

to be passed through. Some form
of breathing. You get wrenched into
and even a roach's eyes reflect. One more

long stare could leave us blind, Annie,
my forehead wants your forehead.
Moving my lips to your name they split.

At the Puppet Show


Fine. One thin cardboard pirate ship and you
want tickets and here we are. Fine. Annie why

don't you blink when that puppet's in the light?
What to read into your plastic expression, Annie,

he's only pretending at ennui. Don't fall
like a scarecrow's wife for his pulled tragedy—

he is no buccaneer, no sea-souled prince,
no real man, Annie, they're shushing me

but listen he's a palate thick with paints and canvas
can do you no good, Annie, I want you to look at me

and I refuse to turn your head. Turn yourself. I touch
my wrist to your cold jaw, feel my own pulse.

You're not quick for him; let's go. Shall I carry you
lightly through the double-doors, my dear,

the audience be damned? I'll perform a little love
for you. Oh, Annie, your cup of water still full

on the floor, I pick it up, cold and sweating like you
and me, I put my nose to it, Annie, and inhale.

## Let the Happy People Dance

Drinking I believe my legs are ideal, as in,
grounded in the mind and insubstantial, no

heavy things, Annie, no pharmacopeia
of dance so don't feel bad, don't stiffen

all jealous of calf & knee & thigh.
There's nothing I can do that I won't do

with you. We're here to celebrate, Annie,
won't you have me, we told them all

it was your birthday and they came.
Let the happy people dance. Annie

on the couch leaning in when I sit down—
slump over—have you broken me? Annie,

I feel unplugged and no more lonely.
The year-round Christmas lights shining

palely through your jaw like tiny miracles,
Annie are you the true complete one?

It's hot in here and the sweat in patches
on my shirt, Annie, everyone secretes,

but you are sweatless and precise, a dry glow.
Coming through like a word of praise

and—what's that, Annie, muffled
as if broke-jawed, a trickle of signals

leaking from your throat? I lean closer
to listen over the music, so close you'd fog

my glasses if you breathed, Annie,
leaning in, *When you touch me*

*you touch me like a small animal*
*touches its wounds*, oh Annie make me twitch.

# LOVER THREE TO LOVER ONE

Predicament, a choking
feather, flows
from my mouth,
but of betrayal I have
little to say but this:
If you stacked all
your discarded violets
they still wouldn't
form a pair
of hot-blooded hands
to hold me. They were
kindling you crumpled,
and your face
is a nest woven
of the spoken and the not-
yet, and I am
a black egg
tumbling out a tender
little mewing.
I don't want to speak
one more predicament
into your swaddling,
to be one more
nurse in need
of a little tending.
But I can't help
my last-ditch trick:

I wrap you
like a statue in white linen.
You collapse,
granite on granite,
and I am mottled
as the natural
world without you.

# THE HUSBAND IMPOSES HIS PERSISTENCE

The husband imposes his persistence.
From your surface, refuse to refuse

another tender foot, a shoehorn,
a smooth fitted aid. The blue thread

between us is binding. Pretty,
your compression leaves blue threads

weeping down the foot like roots.
More than one grain falling, a funnel,

the hours, autumn, and still the husband,
soapstone heavy. Wrap the shoe

at a steady base, the flux at foot and floor,
all this time your beauty shoved

and bandaged in, you totter.
During landmark times you'll stand

on small and nameless boxes,
and when the sculpture garden

seals us to the river, and later
in the sagging futon, and later

on the avenue of oranges,
and later still severe and blue you're frayed

about your limits. To tie you darling
to the present is a snap of light

falling slowly through a blue thread.
I stand in knowledge of the husband's height

but say he loses himself in growth,
too full of feet to stand your legs upon.

# WAX BIRD

you have no taste
for news the house
covers you thickly
you look for lift
from here the distant
lover doesn't offer
a head's worth of heat
left in your shoulder
candle wax melted
to the table forms
a fat and flightless
bird watching it
your hackles rise
like tiny feathers

\*

the t.v. hasn't spoken
for days and you don't
believe in channels
the world outside
her thrift of self has
left your empty form
kneeling at the closet
whispering nothing loudly
don't think the sense
of smell can lace you

to what matters she's
a false bone wrapped
around your sternum


\*


from your window
you see a small bird
suck the sweat
from tiny pebbles
and spit them out
the same pebbles
worried raw
in her silver beak
over and over as if
a piece of stone
could be renewed

# HEAVEN

And when I asked for a round-trip ticket
she scoffed and scratched her wing.

And dandruff from that wing fell
to my elbow where another head
grew treacherously from the divine.

And I asked how many fish
must a man swim past until *et cetera*.

And the twelve beloved hamsters
of my youth were all present
in infinite plastic spheres
they moved with their paws.

And the honest men
interrogated themselves.
And they found the dirt worthy.
And they sold it.

And my back itches only enough
to satisfy the scratching of it.

And the great orange death breezed
right by us, looking lonely.

And one eye fell with a chopping motion.
And the thirsty world getting older.

And looking around for the Dodos they're
all right here.

And I touched a woman with wings
made of rain
and she moved my hand to where it fit.

And a slow mongoose curled
into her chest, rejecting the ravaged whatever,
and her new body grows, hardens.

And the gates are such worked threads.
And the gates pull one more dim curve.

# LOVE SONG IN A FIT OF GIN

*for Becca*


Dear tender bar, I'm passing toward
outland but wanted to tickle your lobe

with my thin-skinned splay of fingers
so trembly sensitive and reaching at you

before drip-drip-dripping this featherless
me to the wrought-iron bottom

of this stool which is no cage as I'm no
pigeon escaping. You were far too nothing

in the glorious nighttime; our limber
*canción*, abutting the calamitous waves

of daylight, couldn't stop the daylight
in all its ugly from toeing up my eyes

and crossing into them, so now it's here,
honey, on the mahogany where you rested

my head and I'm slip-spilling down tender
bar in the dark keep me cultured and alive

in the glorious crash I'm sparking hard
now come catch me I'm unperched.

# Acknowledgements

I am grateful to the editors of the following journals, who published these poems in these or earlier versions:

*The American Poetry Journal*: "Fracturing as a Kindness to be Mined"
*Bateau*: "Mother Tongue"; "What's There"
*Broadsided*: "Dear Body"
*Buffalo Carp*: "Lover Three to Lover One"
*Clementine*: "Divinity Is Power and Love, Marty"
*Conduit*: "My Field"
*CutBank*: "Here"
*Diagram*: "Exeunt Omnes"
*Forklift, Ohio*: "Blood Diamonds"; "Contra"
*Gulf Coast*: "Eat the Bones of the World"
*Greatcoat*: "I'm with You"; "You Can't Stay Alone"
*H_ngm_n*: "Microburst"
*I Thought I Was New Here*: "At Flower, Gripping"
*Jellyfish Magazine*: "Origins"
*KultureVulture*: "Beck Again"
*LEVELER*: "Interview"
*The New Hampshire Review*: "Blason" (published as "Dirty History"); "New Idioms"
*Pebble Lake Review*: "Communion"
*POOL*: "Purpose"
*Pleiades*: "What Home"
*Rhino*: "Heaven"
*Scarab*: "Wax Bird"
*Spinning Jenny*: "How Do We Avoid Living in Jersey?"; "I Am"
*Subtropics*: "Love Song in a Fit of Gin"
*Thermos*: "Reason for Surrender"; "Sugar Glider"
*Third Coast*: "The Husband Imposes His Persistence"
*Web Conjunctions*: "At the Cathouse"; "Hair"; "If It's Not Coming It Must Be Going Away"

"Heaven" and "New Idioms" were reprinted in *The Southern Poetry Anthology, Volume V: Georgia*. "Here" was reprinted in Redux. "How Do We Avoid Living in Jersey?" was reprinted in the anthology *What's Your Exit?: A Literary Detour through New Jersey*. "My Field" was reprinted in *Word by Word: The Iowa Writers' Workshop 75th Anniversary*. "What's There" was reprinted in Verse Daily. Several of these poems also appeared in the chapbook *A Thread of Hands* (Tilt Press 2010).

Special thanks to all of my friends, colleagues, and mentors who helped bring these poems and this book into being, particularly Andy Stallings, Kevin Gonzalez, Isaac Sullivan, Mary Hickman, Peter Richards, Dean Young, James Galvin, Cole Swensen, and Mark Levine. Thanks to The Iowa Writers' Workshop (particularly Jan, Deb, and Connie), Augustana College, and The University of Georgia for time, space, and support. Thanks to Dream Horse Press and J.P. Dancing Bear for embracing this book. Thanks to my families for their endless faith and encouragement. And to Alicia Rebecca Myers: What's best in here bears your mark.

# About the Author

Dan Rosenberg holds degrees from Tufts University and the Iowa Writers' Workshop. He is a Ph.D. student at The University of Georgia in Athens, GA, and a co-editor of *Transom*.

CPSIA information can be obtained at www.ICGtesting.com
Printed in the USA
LVOW080852180712

290551LV00003B/19/P